The Grand Disguise

A Practicing Doctor's
Analysis of Healthcare

William C. Waters III, MD, MACP

Eklektik Press
Atlanta, Georgia

THE GRAND DISGUISE:
A Practicing Doctor's Analysis of Healthcare

Second Edition

Copyright © 1998 by William C. Waters, III, MD
All rights reserved. Eklektik Press, Atlanta, Georgia
Manufactured in the United States of America
by Quill Publications, Columbus, Georgia.

International Standard Book Number 0-9668593-0-8

Library of Congress Catalog Card Number 98-92289

"Why," asked the boy, *"has the price of bread gone up only six times in the last half-century, while the cost of medical care has gone up 40 times . . . with the same housewife shopping for both?"*

"Because," answered the old man, *"the housewife used her own money for the bread."*

Healthcare in America is a huge, expensive structure with constantly appearing defects requiring incessant patching. Some 50 years ago the footings were poured askew; hence cracks appear in the walls, the roof leaks, the floors sag. Repair bills are enormous, and the house is never right. In this paper I contend that to make it plumb will require a careful look at the foundation, then another half-century of structural renovation. A rebuilding project, if it takes place, will demand major commitment and massive effort on the part of the public and its elected representatives. The problem with the sagging house is not the subcontractors, not the builders, not even the developers; the problem is the architectural conception.

This little book maintains that the basis of our difficulty and its origins have largely been overlooked; that they are not mysterious; and that, once they are faced, the solution surfaces as a matter of common sense. The roots are two conceptual errors: first, the Tragic Flaw in reasoning, which presumes that consumers and providers of healthcare will utilize only what is needed even when unlimited resources are made available — that, in other words, the laws of human nature can somehow be suspended by taking a vote. The second, the Grand Disguise, traces what happens when consumers and providers are both protected from the costs — indeed, are denied even the knowledge — of these expenditures.

The remedy: apply logic and remove the mask. An evolutionary process to reach our present undesirable juncture has required 50 years; the long road back, if we take it, will be just as long. One overwhelming problem is that the American political process, geared to the here and now, will have difficulty renovating its perspective to the long view. If it is to rescue medicine, however, it must.

The process of care for the sick and prevention of illness in America has received torrential criticism in recent years — from politicians, the press, citizen groups, and even from members of the healthcare industry. They say it provides poor access; it denies the poor (and many of the middle class); it is disorganized; and it consumes too great a fraction, perhaps 14%, of our gross domestic product (GDP). Publicly provided components — Medicare and Medicaid —

are viewed not only as suboptimal systems but as, incidentally, on the verge of bankruptcy. Managed care, that ground swell of industrial austerity, is inspiring distrust among consumers and despair among providers. Healthcare in America, critics keep saying, is "broken."

There are those who say they can fix it, and remedies abound, often transparently linked to the political agenda of the complaining organization or the aspirant to office. These include: leave everything as is ("Hey, it's the world's greatest system"); promote managed care, including capitation; reform the insurance industry; provide "health IRAs"; move to a single payer system. Indeed people with no previous interest in fiscal management have sprung forth as full-blown self-appointed health economists (perhaps the reader would include the present author! But since economists are freely commenting on medicine, cannot doctors freely comment on economics?).

THE WAY WE ARE

Thus this essay contends that the sources can be identified and a solution formulated. But first — what exactly is the condition of the medical care scene in America?

Whether one reviews multiple polls, consults

the press, reads the healthcare literature, audits "focus groups," or listens to daily conversation in the doctors' lunchroom, several points of agreement about the U. S. health system regularly emerge: the medicine and surgery are generally excellent; the access is difficult for many, especially for the "working poor" or those employed in small business; the cost is high; truly sick people cannot get coverage; and the present delivery system is sorely hampered by interference from outside forces, such as the insurance business, industrial payers, and the government. A far more dire view has just emerged from the Roundtable on Healthcare Quality of the Institute of Medicine. Its consensus statement in September, 1998, claims that medicine in America is a veritable panoply of overuse, underuse, and misuse, and that reengineering is urgently needed. (This amazing pronouncement may be somewhat leavened by a review of the participants of the Roundtable — more than a score of academics, government officials, and industrial representatives, and only a single practicing physician.)

The practitioner's job may actually be even more difficult than it appears to the patient. The consumer, to be sure, knows that health plan requirements must be met, that forms must be executed, that the doctor seems harried and constrained at times. Yet this same user of the system has often been the very one to make the selection she's* concerned about. She surveyed a menu of opportunities provided by her employer and ended up choosing the one which entails the least personal cost and yet generates the most problems. She picked the cheap one. And more and more often this is the HMO option.

But on the other side of the desk or examining table, the physician must deal with as many as 40 different plans, each with its own coverage, its unique fee system, its requirements for referral, its limitations on tests, its proscriptions against hospitalization, its own formulary of drugs. He's harassed by the need to hire new personnel to handle administrative tasks at a time when overhead is climbing and fees are plummeting. The primary care physician as "gatekeeper" may, in capitated contracts, be chagrined to learn there is an apparent reward system for minimizing services. Imagine the patient's alarm on discovering this — that the physician's contract is not with him or her but with some fiscal intermediary which is paying the doctor to reduce care. The impact on the physician-patient relationship is not salutary.

---

* For convenience, *he* and *his* are used for the physician (since most are still male) and *she* and *her* are used for the patient since women predominate in the medical office and hospital and since they are reputed to make 90% of consumer healthcare decisions.

CRITICAL ELEMENT

What early structural error could have led to these defects? Although I propose that this pathologic algorithm began in the 1940s with a defect in reasoning, the critical mover and shaker is now firmly with us: the stunning cost of medical care.

In 1950 national expenditures for health care were not carefully tabulated but must have been relatively trivial, since official figures for 1960 were only $26.9 billion. The bill for 1997 exceeded $1 trillion (1.173) — nearly a 40-fold increase. Inflation during this time, to be sure, has been significant but represents only about a six-time magnification. Medical cost, in gross terms, has thus outpaced the economy nearly seven to one.

Industry has, to say the least, taken note of this spiral. Confronted with 15-22% annual increases in the health bill, big business has reacted. Human resources executives have found themselves saddled with an onerous task every year: telling governing boards that big increases are on the way and, even worse, that the amount is not even known. Thus they have become creative. They have invented something called managed care. This phrase is widely recognized as a filmy euphemism for taking the decision-making process of medicine and surgery away from health professionals and patients and placing it in the hands of business people. That way, presumably, costs can be controlled. The doctors didn't do it; now we will. Beginning predominantly in the west and north, the tidal wave of managed care has flooded the nation. In the most "mature" markets, like San Diego County, 85% of commercial medical care is prepaid, or capitated — in other words, deals are cut ahead of time. Three thousand miles east, in Atlanta, a previously traditional medical city, managed care accounted for 10% of the dollars in 1990 but telescoped the process, and, by 1997, amounted to about 85%, with 20-25% capitation.

Since cost is the fountainhead of the problem, it may be useful to review the mechanisms of payment and their results.

HOW MEDICINE IS PAID FOR

There are now six basic ways medical services are compensated: self-pay (a near-anachronism); indemnity insurance; major medical policies, discounted fee for service; capitation; and government options, notably Medicare.

Self-Pay. In Britain, about 8% of medical costs derive from out-of-pocket sources — the "Harley Street" option. Surprisingly, and despite our relative affluence, only about 4% of Americans pay their own medical bills from personal funds. Britons of course have as an alternative to private funding only the National Health Service with its cursory exams and its long delays for elective surgery, particularly major procedures; Americans have the long menu of options detailed here and the relatively convenient services offered. The advantage of the self-pay mechanism is the preservation of control by the patient and doctor; the problem is that in America costs have now accelerated to the point where few are willing — or able — to pay the bill.

Indemnity insurance. This traditional health policy provides for most services, usually offering to cover 80% of "usual and customary charges" after a deductible and providing similar or even higher payment for extended hospitalizations. The premium for such instruments nowadays is dear — as much as $6000 per year for a healthy family of three — so that both employers and employees alike are understandably demurring on this option. Indeed, the indemnity policy is rapidly fading from the scene; in advanced managed care areas such as urban California, it is said to occupy only 2% of the market. One healthcare manager there said, "We can't actually find anybody with one of these policies."

Major medical. In a serious or prolonged illness — once a basic "deductible" amount of cost is met — the major medical policy takes over and usually covers well the frequently astronomical bills which accumulate. The problem is that the first $2000-5000 must be borne by the patient, and Americans are not used to coming up with cash for medical expenses. (This is the Grand Disguise incarnate; the patient, or employee, is indeed paying for it but doesn't seem to know it. See below.)

Discounted fee for service. In an effort to control costs, or even to make annual rises in rates more predictable, insurance companies negotiate discounted contracts with hospitals and doctors. Generally, they pick and choose hospitals, electing the one which agrees to the lowest figure. Similarly, they try different physicians, selecting those who will accept a 20%, or 40%, reduction from customary levels. Such insurance firms may parade their selectivity as elitism; one recently filled billboards with the motto "We check the histories of our doctors." Indeed, they do check — their histories of compliance with the best deal. Solo practitioners may find themselves victims of the process called "cherry-picking," in which individual doctors try to negotiate with powerful payers such as insurance companies — accounting for the popularity of group provider organizations.

Capitation. This form is based on a fixed per-person prepayment. It may cover all services — "global" capitation — or may arrange certain "carve-outs" such as cardiac services. It is important because of its rapid ascendance throughout the country. Indeed, most consultants continue with the belief that it will rapidly become the dominant compensation mechanism, despite more recent public demand for choice in the marketplace. In this modality the healthcare organization, including the physician, receives payment on, say, the 10th of every month whether the patient has been seen or not, treated or not, hospitalized or not. On the west coast, which has led the way in managed care, overwhelming "penetrance" by prepayment of the commercial insurance marketplace is common. In highly developed areas, the payment has been screwed down to remarkably low levels — $85 per member per month for global coverage in some places, with the insurance company sequestering 25% of that for "administrative costs."

Medicare. The over-65 population, if not employed full time, are not candidates for commercial insurance. They can't get it. They automatically receive Medicare Part A (mainly hospital services) and, if they wish insured doctors' services, will accept and pay for Part B. There are strict rules governing physician and hospital reimbursement, tight guidelines for utilization,

14

and prohibitions against physicians' standard fees. Medicine at the moment is one of the few industries in America in which prices are fixed.* (These strictures are described in "The Patient Catches the Doctor's Disease.")

HOW IT'S GOING

The impact of managed care on the actual quality of medicine is difficult to quantitate. Health plan managers, not unexpectedly, maintain that outcomes are as good or better under HMOs. Hard data, collected by impartial assessors, are scanty. Generally, healthy young families with few medical needs seem pleased, while those with serious problems report heavy roadblocks. Recent major surveys at Harvard and by Care-Data Reports, Inc., showed big dips in satisfaction with HMOs over the last two years. Quality assessments, carried out most extensively in Philadelphia and on the west coast, find considerable variation, although critics question the criteria. Interestingly, a difference in "quality" among providers has not seemed to sway payers in their selection of plans.

---

*Others include travel agents, taxi drivers, utilities, and rent in some areas.

Informal opinion on this subject, however, is not wanting. Individual patients and physicians regularly complain that optimal care is not possible when the physician is "graded" on his austerity rather than his medical powers. Certainly any doctor confronting patients who are adapting to the sea change in delivery of care will report the anxiety they show — Will I now get second-class care? Am I now in a medical mill? Is this a clinical interview or a negotiation?

WHAT THE PATIENT THINKS

By far the larger share of negative assessments has been leveled at the pre-paid, or capitated, method of sponsoring medical care, with "providers" and "consumers" alike voicing dissatisfaction. (Both, by the way, complain about using these "provider-consumer" market terms for the traditionally sacrosanct doctor-patient relationship.) Patients are either given no choice about their "new plan" or are allowed to select from a menu of options. Then they are told to pick a "primary care physician" (PCP) from a list, usually either an internist or a family practitioner, who will now serve as their "gate-keeper," or entry point into the healthcare system. The patient must contact this physician, or his office, every time any problem arises to obtain a referral for an eye doctor, a gynecologist, dermatologist, ortho-

16

pedist, etc. The PCP may be new to the "member," or in some cases the patient finds she can select her long-standing doctor if the latter has agreed to participate in the new plan. Frequently it is alarming for the individual to learn that she has undergone a metamorphosis in the same office from patient to consumer, and that her long-term friend is now behaving more like a supplier than a doctor. Many offices are reporting distress, or even terror, on the part of new patients, afraid they cannot get proper care in this unaccustomed system.

Anecdotes of unprecedented behavior abound: for example, the patient whose first act during her first ever telephone call with the receptionist was to start screaming; and the young woman who had her benefits manager contact the medical office because the doctor didn't call her back within 45 minutes (she proved to have a cold of three days' duration). This anxiety, or even panic, seems to derive from the fear that the physician is now being rewarded for his rationing skills rather than for his expertise and concern — a fear which unfortunately may sometimes be grounded in fiscal fact.

Complaints surface daily about the failure of employers, insurance companies, or HMOs to educate their consumers regarding the provisions of these plans. It is routine for patients to appear at a doctor's office unaware of even their type of health insurance, much less its provisions. Learning that routine blood work, electrocardiogram, and chest x-ray will not be included in their capitated coverage for the "periodic health exam," they express stark amazement. Told for the first time that they cannot go to the ear-nose-throat doctor without "permission" from the PCP, or that plastic surgery is probably not covered at all, they become furious. And this anger is not characteristically directed at the HMO or employer (whose brochure simply promised "comprehensive coverage") but at the physician or his employees who are the bearers of the unwanted messages. Everyday doctor-patient relationships understandably deteriorate.

It is interesting to speculate why insurance companies and HMOs fail to communicate adequately with their customers about their product — why they don't, for example, make it clear that MRIs, CT scans, endoscopies, or referrals to specialists must be approved by the "case care manager" (a non-MD); why subscribers don't understand they must "sign up" with a primary care doctor; why they must present a co-pay (e. g., $10-20) at the time of the visit. Perhaps the cost of mounting such an educational program is too massive and is thus left to the physician's office. Perhaps calling attention to restrictions carries an anti-marketing effect in a culture used to hearing raves from the purveyor of any service. On the other hand, physicians and person-

18

nel certainly recognize that new managed care patients are themselves in a state of denial: they liked the part about a "$10 physical" but decided not to read the rest of the pamphlet.

More than ever, the pressure of reduced compensation (see below) impels the physician to increase his minute-to-minute efficiency. Managed care markedly exaggerates the ancient number-one complaint of patients, expressed in every survey over at least 60 years, that the doctor "doesn't spend enough time," or doesn't listen closely enough. The doctor, particularly the primary-care physician, must speed through the daily list of patients; many consultants agree that a 50% increase in volume is needed to sustain viable income levels in such an office.

Nowhere is this new alienation more obvious than in the case of telephone calls. Since overhead is high and climbing, and since time on the phone is not reimbursed at all, the telephone conversation with the physician in areas with high managed care penetration has all but evaporated. PAs and nurses deal with messages or, at best, medical assistants pass them to the physicians and back to patients. As telephone calls triple and quadruple, vociferous complaints are often received about voicemail or "not being able to get through" to office personnel.

This resistance to electronic devices is somewhat

ironic and underlines the highly personal nature of the medical interaction, for the automated technique of phone answering is of course well accepted in home and office alike. Patients have been known to complain loudly to the tape that they "want the doctor, not the damned machine, and would you please have him call, and if I'm not here, leave a message on my voicemail!" But medical office workers, inundated by the barrage of increased calls regarding referrals, confirmation of coverage, and billing, are simply unable to provide, on demand, the much-desired human voice. More phone lines would require more personnel and hence more overhead at precisely a time when costs beg to be reduced. Staff members, confronted with confused, concerned, and even irate patients have been known to comment that "We now hate our jobs." Also overheard: "We used to kid about the salt mine. Now it *is* a salt mine."

Cognizant of the new system or not, patients may — and possibly should — complain about reduced services. Markets undergoing accelerated managed care have seen impressive declines in certain functions: as much as 40% drops in utilization of medical endoscopy, arthroscopy, and cardiac catheterization have followed introduction of "risk contracting" with integrated delivery systems in some areas; consultations with specialists have fallen off dramatically; surgical therapies such as coronary bypass may be averted or delayed in favor of less expensive treatments such as drug management. These reductions are, of course, at the very heart of the savings engendered by managed care. The net effect on health of such changes continues to be a source of debate: Was too much surgery being performed in the first place, or is too little now being done? Was colonoscopy carried out too liberally, or is this accepted method of preventing colon cancer now being rationed too severely?

A concerned citizen might wonder too that one of the improvements touted during the managed care fervor of the Clinton health bill — amelioration of the uninsured rate — has not been borne out (14% then, 17% now); and in highly "mature" areas, the fraction of the populace "going bare" of any medical insurance has risen rather than fallen (to 45% in some places).

To be sure, Medicare, the original brand of managed, or monitored, care, had to some extent prepared the ground. Older patients had begun to get used to premature discharges — or prohibitions against admission at all for some procedures, such as cataract extractions. Admitted medical patients have been routinely required to receive IV fluids (at a "minimum" of 75 ml/hr) in order to meet Medicare guidelines — some perhaps unnecessarily, some perhaps with some risk, most without knowing the real reason for such invasive therapy. The patient who is dissatisfied with the system and requests to pay his physician out of pocket for "first class care" is restrained by means of a skillfully crafted federal mechanism in which the physician is "guilty" if he accepts more than prescribed fees, or if he contracts privately with one patient while following Medicare rules with others. Congress has lately extended the penalties for such trespasses (see below).

Frequently Medicare patients have found themselves unwelcome in internists' and family practitioners' offices — in one metro area at last count only 10% of internists were taking new Medicare patients. On the other hand, as commercial managed care fee allowances have been progressively ratcheted down, Medicare rates are looking better and better; some hospital adminstrators in western states are now calling Medicare "the gold standard."

An unfortunate — some patients say intolerable — consequence of Medicare/managed care intervention is the virtual elimination of confidentiality. To be sure, insurance people, HCFA officials, doctors, and hospital administrators correctly point out that, strictly speaking, medical records remain private until and if the patient authorizes, in writing, their release. But wait: the patient does so in every case, up front; otherwise, no coverage — insurance companies, HMOs, government must inspect diagnoses and records as a

22

condition of payment of claims. So a patient's depression and sexually transmitted diseases become essentially public. A recent report suggests that 37% of psychiatrists and psychologists in Santa Clara County have one or more patients who elect to pay out of pocket to avoid opening their private diaries.

On the other hand, the citizen who has been so unwise as to pass his/her 65th birthday does not have this privilege: private contracting on government-covered services is against the law for the practitioner in America (see FIXING THE FAULT LINES).

Another consequence of this unconditional release of information is the doctor's growing reluctance to record everything. Knowing his records will be tossed into the public arena, he may simply leave out the story about the alcohol and the impotence, thereby truncating the all-important medical history and denigrating its value.

Perhaps the most disconcerting feature of managed care which should concern the "consumer" is the economic disenfranchisement of the truly sick patient. If the ill person is covered by deep discounted fee for service in a commercial or Medicare plan, will her multiple problems be adequately dealt with in the busy office or the hospital? If a prepaid plan is in force, will the physician expend critical hours of time with a complex set of problems when his pay (perhaps $9-$15 per patient per month) is unaffected by his efforts? The author, an internist accustomed to complicated patients over the years, submitted one day's problem lists of patients to one of his U. S. senators and asked how could he properly handle his daily load of, say, 25-30 of these cases in the new era? The senator's reply: "You can't, Bill, you can't."

THE PATIENT CATCHES
THE DOCTOR'S ILLNESS

The patient-physician relationship is necessarily personal, subjective, intimate, and typically involves a worried, even alarmed, "customer" hoping for clarification, reassurance, or at least palliation from a calm, concerned, but objective professional. It is not a long stretch to imagine that a patient will be adversely affected if her trusted advisor's self-esteem has been lately damaged. Anxiety, or even anger, may replace the physician's traditional equanimity after receiving directives from as many as 40 different plans, after experiencing a halving of income, or facing the prospect of becoming a salaried employee after years of self-direction. Many patients complain that their doctor spends half the interview time talking about managed care; this turn of events does not reassure them.

Polls and informal conversations with MDs regularly generate a litany of complaints about the new "economical" system.

The obstacle of preadmission certification constantly surfaces in the discounted payment system: here the patient cannot enter the hospital except in a real emergency without permission from the "system" — i. e., a "manager," or clerk, must determine that the anticipated admission meets predetermined criteria. Sometimes the permission-giver cannot be reached for hours or days. This individual, who may be completely untrained as a health professional, may well misunderstand the diagnosis and mistakenly disallow the hospitalization. At times the decision not to pay comes later, during or after the hospital stay. On the other hand, daily calls to the doctor during hospitalization are routine, asking if the patient "can't go home today or at least be discharged early tomorrow."*

---

*One surgeon was paged in the hospital by an insurance clerk wanting to know why a hernia patient had not already been sent home. The doctor replied that the operation had only been completed within minutes, the patient was still recovering from general anesthesia in the operating room, and in any event was 85 years old and might require overnight observation. The extra day was disallowed ("did not meet criteria"). The patient, who happened to be a prominent businessman and former mayor of a large metropolitan city, paid out of pocket, but voiced displeasure with the system.

If "inadequate" explanations are offered, the doctor may get a call from an assistant medical director, himself an MD not in active practice, requesting reasons for continued inpatient services. Many practicing physicians question the backgrounds of these "insurance doctors" and understandably wonder how, in any event, a professional could call shots on management without ever seeing the patient or his chart.* Collegiality at times deteriorates and angry confrontations even occur. One internist was criticized for "unprofessional" comments to an insurance doctor on the telephone; he later received a letter from the medical director confirming that "review of the recorded conversation" indeed confirmed "inappropriate language." (Later a prominent local law firm declared the recording to be legal even though obtained without consent.)

On the other hand, recent reports state that denials are much less frequent than expected — averaging only 1-2% in some systems. But the threat of this type of activity, together with the financial incentives for "economy" of care, must be potent, if one looks at the profound fall in hospital days and procedures. Health insurance organizations have sent written directives to physicians requiring that they "not discuss" with patients expensive therapies such as renal trans-

---

*See note on previous page.

plantation without specific permission from the plan. At least one large southern HMO has sent an admonition to its physician-participants threatening sanctions if any of a long list of procedures and tests are even *mentioned* to the patient without prior approval (which may require 72 hours). In other words, if the family doctor seeing a patient with a backache — or stomachache — merely *suggests* before approval from headquarters that an MRI — or an endoscopy — might be indicated, he does so at his personal economic peril. Such "gag rules" are now being addressed by federal legislation, and some states (e.g., Georgia) have outlawed the practice.

"Primary care physician (PCP)," a much-derided term for the family doctor, internist, or family practitioner, identifies the person who sees the patient first; and the insurance company or HMO has placed upon him, with a minimum of subtlety, the task of curbing services.

PCPs complain of being "speed-breakers" in the medical/financial process. The doctor has as many as 40 bulky manuals in his office, each containing rules for dealing with patients under that particular plan. Inspections are held: employees with laptop computers spend the day, "auditing" the office and its professionals on topics from documentation of date of birth to last menstrual period. This function, which will be carefully cited in the HMO's advertising as a "quality survey," is necessarily carried out by individuals with limited educational background. One doctor complained that "a high-school graduate" was grading the performance of his three-MD group whose total medical education and experience exceeded 100 years.

Another grading system receiving still more comments is the "report card" issued by managed care agencies to primary doctors, frequently assigning them a position on the "curve" among their peers. This is the curve not of clinical excellence but of fiscal frugality: did the doctor hold drug costs, referrals, and hospitalizations to a minimum? If so, a reward from the bonus pool is coming. If not, the plan will make no such payment and the physician's record will suffer.

On the other hand, some firms conduct *two* audits — one for economics and one for "quality." Ironically, high performance on one may cause low performance on the other. In any event, with enough bad grades, the doctor may find himself "deselected" — i. e., dropped from the plan; patients seeing him under that program will need to find a new doctor when the current contract runs out. The physician will lose a percentage of his practice, provoking many to restrict commitments so that not more than 15% of revenue comes from a single plan (HMOs do not like to cooperate with this limitation, since they gain bargaining power when they control a larger fraction of a practitioner's business). Many contracts between physicians and health organizations permit the latter to cancel without cause; some state medical societies are challenging these arrangements in court.

The patient in modern America at times may also wonder if the man across the desk or examining table is haunted — and hence distracted — by the fear of malpractice. Indeed claims across the nation have never been higher nor awards greater, despite sporadic legislative efforts at the state level. The legal liability problem surely has escalated costs by provoking excessive tests and expanded documentation (see *Zoom Factor*). More recently the development of managed care has sounded new alarm bells: Will curbs on diagnostic procedures and the rushing of the clinical interview increase the number of suits? No systematic study is available, but two of the large national carriers report that capitation clearly accelerates malpractice risk and makes defense more difficult, and seminars by lawyers at healthcare centers are multiplying ominously. One prominent metropolitan plaintiff's attorney, asked if he thought capitation would downgrade the standard of care — and hence increase claim opportunities — replied, "Yes, indeed" (with a perceptible smile). Another said, "It should be a real boon for my business." In a number of instances large HMOs have paid huge awards because of "withholding care."

Concerned physicians have provided further evidence of reaction to the managed care epidemic through Defend Health Care, an organization spearheaded by Dr. Bernard Lown, in Boston. They hope to provide standards for HMO performance, but policing of a process driven in another direction by monetary goals is always difficult. In December, 1997, this organization sponsored the "Boston Tea Party," a demonstration by doctors and patients against the requirements of regulated medicine.

On no sectors of the profession has managed care had a greater demoralizing effect than upon the surgeons and specialists. With gatekeeper screening, "deselection," deep discounts, and non-coverage of many procedures, incomes of invasive cardiologists and gastroenterologists have plummeted. Early retirements have soared. As the process has moved, like the weather, from west to east and north to south, so have specialists moved to more promising, easterly and southerly, locations.

This flight pattern is of course limited: one consultant, working in Baltimore, Maryland, commented that the local neurosurgeons and plastic surgeons now had no place to go "except the Atlantic." In an effort to get around the system, specialists have formed "horizontal networks" — for example, of urologists or oncologists — to contract directly with payers, but experience to this point suggests these entities die out as comprehensive "vertically integrated systems" emerge. One large multi-specialty direct-referral organization, much touted because of its wide consumer choice, has experienced losses and severe downdrafts on Wall Street recently. In July, 1997, it was reported that as much as 10-15% of radiologists, pathologists, anesthesiologists, and plastic surgeons remained unemployed — *no job at all* — one full year after completing training. At the other end of the career spectrum, a seminar was held in Amelia Island, Florida, in October, 1997, entitled "Life after Orthopedics," designed to describe alternatives for those prematurely leaving the bone-and-joint profession. It sold out at 500 physicians-attendees and so another session was scheduled in Texas. This also sold out promptly after achieving an attendance list of 500.

Surveys indicate an alarming disenchantment on the part of physicians. Many say they would make a different choice if they had to do it over again. Some have retired early, and many more appear to be considering it. Insurance people say that the physician has changed from a premiere candidate for a disability policy to a high-risk prospect: he is looking, they say, for any excuse to quit. In addition to this individual loss of morale, hospital medical directors and physicians themselves report a progressive decline in collegiality among their ranks. Specialists grow wary of primary care doctors, suspicious that they are holding back referrals; independent PCPs resent hospitals' employing platoons of doctors to compete with them; independent practice associations (IPAs) wrestle with health maintenance organizations (HMOs); and the luncheon conversation in the doctors' dining room veers away from interesting patients, golf, fishing, and family — to managed care and its perceived horrors.

Education directors decry the decline of attendance at regular professional educational conferences. One institution sent out a survey asking why. The results suggested that managed care concerns were the reason, although some doctors felt that interest in continuing medical education may resurface after the "tidal wave" had passed. The effect of Medicare and managed care on total MD scholarship has not been systematically assessed, but some educators feel that it is disastrous.

THE PATIENT FEELS THE HOSPITAL'S PAIN

It is common knowledge that hospitals are reacting to the shrinkage of the healthcare dollar, and some of the measures taken affect the patient directly. Closure of the hospital itself may deprive the patient of her favorite medical center. Most hospitals which lock their doors are located in already underserved areas. Almost all facilities which remain open are "closing beds" — i.e., destaffing acute care areas and turning them into something else, like administrative space (needed, by the way, to handle the accelerated paper chase). Many community hospitals are "gobbled up" by big for-profit organizations with huge cash reserves; the "bought" facility may now adopt an abruptly unfamiliar, stand-offish business philosophy. Or, much to the surprise of the local populace, it may abruptly announce it is closing as a "strategic move" (but only, of course, after the managers have carefully plugged the book price of the hospital into Wall Street's valuation of the parent company).

Perhaps more alarming is the "downsizing" of services which the local hospital — whether not-for-profit or investor-owned — must undergo to survive. Since the biggest cost is personnel, and since the most expensive personnel are professionals, the nurse/patient ratio must shrink. Lesser-trained people, such as nursing assistants, must now take over functions previously performed by RNs. The health industry has labeled these and other changes as the "transformation of medical care delivery" — a more palatable phrase for saving money by reducing the level of expertise applied to any given service.

Consolidations occur: hospitals A, B, and C condense their billing, accounting, laboratory, laundry, management and other pieces into single central units, leaving only token representatives at the local level. These consortia hope to control costs by large-scale purchasing and consolidation (and gain the advantages of mass contracting), but patients perceive a loss of the personal touch in what is certainly a personal part of their lives.

One might ask: Why should hospitals have to resort to such penurious measures? The reasons are good ones — they have seen a reduction in patients' length of stay, in admissions, and in reimbursement for services — what administrators are calling the "triple whammy." As much as 40-60% reduction in hospital occupancy has occurred or is expected. Hospital days per thousand Medicare patients have plummeted to one-third of previous levels in many areas. Not-for-profit hospitals, which require a 3-5% margin for renewal of facilities, are struggling to meet payrolls and other current expenses. The investor-owned systems are publicly declaring their goal of reducing "medical loss ratios" — a *Wall Street Journal* term for money "squandered" on patient care instead of being "efficiently" returned to the stockholder.

Medicare in the '70's had already devised a system of "DRGs" — Diagnosis Related Groups — which provides for payment by diagnosis rather than cost or length of stay. Thus an admission for a hemorrhage from a peptic ulcer will usually garner the same payment whether the patient stays a day or a month; a heart attack requiring three days' stay may elicit the same reimbursement as a three-week hospitalization. The authors of the DRG plan received awards for their cleverness; some of our more marginal hospitals have closed because of it.

TRYING TO FIX THE FAULT LINES

As the house of healthcare has settled on its flawed foundations, and as cracks have appeared in the walls, building managers have attempted repairs. In an effort to prevent further soaring costs in the early 70's, the Nixon administration instituted price controls, only to see expenditures rebound steeply and "catch up" in the next few years. The American Medical Association (AMA) urged members in 1983 to "freeze" fees for one year. In 1984 Congress authorized the Health Care Financing Administration (HCFA) to halt the annual habit of adjusting Medicare rates to the Consumer Price Index. Thus physician's fees for the over-65 population have been permitted to rise only a cumulative 8% from 1984-1997 while average commercial fees have risen about 150% and CPI has climbed about 90% during this interval. (Physicians who complied with the AMA dictum had their "profiles" frozen and suffered still greater fiscal losses.) Yet since physicians' charges constitute less than 20% of the bill, healthcare unsurprisingly continued its double-digit rise each year. DRGs were instituted, as indicated above, with damage to some institutions and benefits to others, but with an inadequate control of the Medicare cost picture.

The Clinton Health Plan, outlined in more than 1400 pages, had as part of its essential thrust the encouragement of "managed competition." Though the bill failed in Congress, observers noted that managed care had accelerated apace anyway. Then, as the evils of this system have become evident, Congressmen, mainly from the Democrat side of the central aisle, have offered more than 20 other bills to "correct" managed care. President Clinton has proposed a "Patient's Bill of Rights for Healthcare" containing prohibitions which, if instituted, would partially obstruct the very process he had earlier advocated.

On the Republican side, Norwood and D'Amato earlier presented a plan which virtually puts managed care in reverse: a major medical consulting firm estimated that, if adopted, this bill would raise national healthcare costs by a startling 23%. As recently as July, 1998, the House of Representatives passed a

Republican-sponsored bill imposing many sanctions on HMOs and insurance companies, but even this instrument failed to change the rule that only doctors, not payers, can be sued for malpractice, allowing the insurance companies to continue to make medical management decisions. This deploring of the HMO option may be only an academic exercise anyway, since 1997 saw 57% of 506 of these organizations reporting a net loss.

Still more impressive is the financial distress evident by early 1998: Kaiser, granddaddy and oft-cited role model of the HMO movement, slipped from earnings of $265 million in 1996 to losses of $270 million in 1997. Others — Aetna and PacifiCare — reported disappointing results; Oxford Health Plans reported a big loss — its first. Apparently these companies have applied conventional equine harnesses to the healthcare animal, only to discover that they are dealing with a rhinoceros.

A recent Presidential proposal to extend Medicare backwards a few years to younger people makes one wonder: if we have created a shanty, shall we now acquire more shanties — and create a shantytown? Mortar had been applied to cover the rents in the brick; this mortar itself had cracked; and now painting is recommended, presumably to improve the appearance. Nothing is new here: T. S. Eliot wrote, in *The*

Hollow Men, "Humankind cannot stand very much reality...."

Not only had the price of healthcare grown too large for the private pocketbook, even the tariff for health insurance seemed unaffordable unless paid by an employer. People moving from job to job might lose coverage, so COBRA provisions were introduced. Even here the price to the individual was high during the unemployed interval. Enter: the Kassebaum-Kennedy Bill. Touted as the "Health Insurance Portability and Accountability Act of 1996," this initiative compels insurers to continue coverage despite job changes and major illnesses — inadvertently damping further the original intent of managed care, and by the way further hamstringing attempts to make the medical business cost-effective.

This bill did not address the far greater problem — that of the uninsured — and recent reports indicate a rise in the "uncovered" population from 14.8% in 1987 to 17.7% in 1996 — yielding a current figure of 41.4 million. (However, the same report indicates that only 15.8% of citizens are uninsured compared with 44% of non-citizens.) Ironically, efforts to "fix" the insurance situation may have made things worse, as 16 states with the most reforms saw their uninsured rate rise by eight times as much as the other states; some companies abandoned insurance plans altogether; and some insurance firms simply "left town."

But most dramatic (though little publicized) was the last one-third of this bill, which, as editorials in the *Wall Street Journal* and elsewhere suggest, tend to criminalize the medical profession. "Mistakes" in coding, intentional or not, can be punished by fines of triple damages, plus $10,000 and/or 10 years in prison for each infraction. If a "pattern" of variance is "detected" penalties can be extrapolated over the doctor's entire practice — not only the Medicare portion, but, surprisingly, the commercial part as well. Several years ago a midwestern nephrology group was told they owed 12 million dollars because of upcoding of dialysis procedures. After some three years this penalty was downgraded by the courts to $800,000 plus $1,000,000 in community service. Amounts of legal fees were not released.

More recently an FBI swat team in full regalia including flak jackets invaded a southern small-town doctor's office during business hours. The physician had received no prior notice but the local newspaper and TV had, and they were present in force with cameras working. The agents scooped up charts and left the impression that there was a possible coding issue, but at the time of this writing no actual charges had been made — by HCFA, that is; the populace of the small town may have come to their own conclusions, and the doctor must be wondering about his practice.

Among the more demeaning aspects of the Kassebaum-Kennedy Bill is the tone of this section applicable to physicians. Legal consultants describe the language as "lifted in a piece from earlier legislation directed at drug dealers." Demoralizing, too, was the unanimity of opinion in the Congress: the House passed it overwhelmingly and the Senate 100-0. The some 800,000 physicians in the U. S. must wonder where to look for political representation, since the most frequent charges under attack as "fraudulent" in the primary-care office are only in the $26-76 range. (This "picking-on" the doctor became less palatable when, in summer, 1998, the Senate voted 65-35 not to place caps on attorney's fees which were reported to be as much as $92,000 per hour in one of the government-sponsored tobacco cases).

Perhaps the Congress, discouraged by the ineffectiveness of sanctions against drug lords (whose careers, after all, are already dedicated to law-breaking), had turned to more fertile and satisfying ground: the doctors, who have a record of carefully and obsequiously obeying every ordinance.

To show they were serious the Congress authorized increased funds for chart audit, empowered the FBI to intervene with 450 dedicated agents, and enlisted the Inspector General in the process. Consultants report that the FBI agents will be CPAs with no medical or technical terminology background but a four-to-six-week course in the new documentation guidelines. Apparently they will need no search warrants (presumably "probable cause" has been established by the doctor's profile pattern).

On the other hand, HHS Chief Donna Shalala has requested Congress to authorize agents to carry guns and issue warrants when necessary. With $400 million allocated to the audit process, they are expected to recover $23 for each dollar expended. Interesting, too, is the fact that office staff members will now be liable for the same penalties as the doctor but can be immunized if they choose to "cooperate" in the audit. If so, they will be further rewarded with 25% of any proceeds obtained through fines and refunds. Moreover, any "tips" they give the agents about other practices which later prove fruitful will garner the same 25% bonus.

HCFA developed new documentation guidelines for physicians in May, 1997. These new mandates filled 56 pages and directed the physician in exactly how many items must be written or dictated into each record in order to recover the basic Medicare payment and, furthermore, escape criminal prosecution. (A new revision was promised after a ground swell of protest among America's doctors, but preliminary drafts of the new "framework" released by AMA suggested that Band-aids, rather than radical surgery, had been utilized.) The cost of the additional time spent writing down or dictating and transcribing negative statements (e.g., "patient reports no headache, staggering, numbness, tingling, weakness of extremities," etc., in a healthy patient reporting for, say, abdominal complaints) is impossible to calculate. One doctor, attending a conference on coding, said, "It's like making the journalists diagram all their sentences or go to jail." Already, before the new and more cumbersome system appeared, an urban cardiologist — known for good documentation — had complained that his office received $26 for a single office visit from Medicare and the transcription bill was $24 (not counting office overhead expense, personnel, or, of course, any physician salary).

Although most of these activities were not scheduled to begin until early 1998 the Office of the Inspector General had already dutifully started executing its assignment: it published results of a survey showing that some 20% of all Medicare health bills were "overcharges," primarily based on "inadequate documentation." Mr. Stark promptly ascribed the discrepancies to "criminal behavior." With some 10,000 possible codes accompanied by descriptors which are regarded by many in the industry as vague, it is interesting that the survey apparently found no "undercodings" — just "overcodings." Yet medical management consultants comment that doctors tend to downgrade, rather than upcode, their services for fear of reprisal.

The first formal survey on coding practices conducted by HCFA on a national basis had taken place in 1991. Obtaining charts on a random basis and reviewing the documentation against the codes, the agency had concluded that 40% of codes were "incorrect." A more extensive prepayment survey of one percent of claims, completed in early 1998, resulted in a 40% total rejection rate and another 20% downcoding (thus 60% "incorrect"). Here again apparently no "undercodings" were "discovered." Something, it appears, will have to be changed — the system, the doctors, or the traditional concept of medical record keeping.

In addition to these CPT codes, which describe the level and type of service given, every bill submitted to Medicare, Medicaid, and some commercial programs must contain one or more ICD-9 codes, which define the complaint or diagnosis. Furthermore, any lab test ordered must be matched to an "acceptable" ICD-9 label, or diagnosis, even though all Medicare lab charges are paid direct to the laboratory and do not involve the physician; otherwise the patient must pay for the procedures (unless the doctor has neglected to have the patient sign a release, in which case the doctor

43

is required to pay for the patient's test).

Efforts to regulate the physician, previously a sacrosanct figure, have been surprisingly successful to date. It has in fact been suggested that denigration of the physician's place in society is part of the strategy (of a co-opting government-insurance complex) to wrest control first of medical costs and then of medicine itself from these once-proud professionals. First degrade the doctor's standing, then any financial or regulatory punishment one metes out will be well received by the public. Call him — let's see — not *scholar, professor, doctor,* but *provider.* Or, oh yes, *vendor.* Go further — call him *supplier.* The President has already announced his plans to charge him a user fee for being a Medicare provider — i. e., for the privilege of submitting to HCFA's bureaucratic regulations and fee reductions.

Why our government should focus all this activity on the ordinary physician-patient encounter is hard to understand from an economic point of view, since total doctor bills account for only 19% of the health bill. In any event, beset with this ill fortune, the physician might well be expected to turn to his medical society for relief, and indeed complaints typically rage on the floors of his county and state medical organizations. But then he realizes that his biggest MD organization, the American Medical Association (AMA), is the very group which has sat down with HCFA to formulate the codes, the coding criteria, and the documentation guidelines. These rules systematically provide fertile ground for the anticipated HCFA audits — not on what the doctors does, not on what he omits, but on what he writes down or dictates. He may wonder indeed if his representative organization has helped set the trap. Membership in AMA, though it has risen slightly in absolute numbers, has fallen in percentage of physicians from 80% in 1960 to 42% in 1996, so that most doctors are now not members. The grass-roots House of Delegates of the AMA, responding to a nationwide MD uproar, in 1997 denounced any "numerical accounting" based on medical records. HCFA responded by saying "They have left us nothing," and suggested that more onerous rules will be forthcoming.

There is talk of unionization and strikes, but several unique obstacles exist. The first is the physician culture: doctors won't deprive their patients and they're too individualistic ("Eagles don't flock" and "You can't herd cats" are familiar comments). Certainly the Canadian experience in the early '70's is hard to ignore: rebelling against the nationalization of medicine, the doctors nonetheless delivered 80% of the usual care during the "strike," which was short-lived anyway. Furthermore, doctors can't qualify for the definition of a union in the U. S. The requirements include: "the individuals must be employed and cannot serve in supervisory roles" and hence the doctors couldn't strike. If they even sit down somewhere and discuss prices they are violating the Sherman Antitrust Act; a number of powerful actions by the Federal Trade Commission against doctors are on record. Legislation in now pending to provide revision of these anti-trust sanctions, but the outlook is uncertain.

Oversight on the expenditure of public funds is, of course, essential, but providers and consumers in the healthcare industry are complaining of what they deem fascist measures. To escape these threatening strictures a physician and patient might well wish to deal one-on-one and forget Medicare, or other controlled payment system, just as a British physician can bypass the National Health System whenever he and the patient agree to do so. Not in America — any doctor who ever treats any patient over 65 under the Medicare rules cannot then contract directly with another on penalty of fine and imprisonment. In order to change over his entire practice to private billing, he is currently required by the newest rules *not to treat any patient under Medicare rules for two years*. Since 96% of doctors work under Medicare laws, and since 30-80% of various practices involve the elderly population, this option appears moot.

An outside observer — say, an astronomer from

another planet — might well think that medicine in 1990's America is a supernova, a transitional star on the brink of either exploding or condensing into a black hole. His questions would be which and when, not whether: This, he would say, is an unstable star. It will change.

And it will.

HAVE WE LEARNED ANYTHING?

Managed care has indeed reduced annual cost rises in the private sector. From 1988 through 1990 the yearly jump was 15-18% per year but, as managed care penetration reached 85% of the workforce, it fell strikingly to an average of 1-2% from 1994 through 1997. However, this bit of frugality has not provoked much celebration in board rooms, since many insurance companies and consultants recognize a progressive disenchantment with the HMO choice and an increasing move to the point-of-service and direct referral method, both of which will be more expensive. The big savings have, they say, already been seen and a steady climb is predicted. Current forecasts by HCFA economists say that doctors' charges will rise from $221 billion in 1998 to $427 billion in 2007, and annual rises in healthcare costs will jump from 2.9% in 1996 to 7.3% in 2000.

Most discouraging of all is the price pattern in the public sector, with Medicare still going up 8-10% and Medicaid 15-20% per year. Thus over-all expenditures have been climbing 5-9% yearly since 1990 and, although 1996 figures for the total reached a low of 4.4%, experts predict that the new rebound is in the offing. HCFA looks forward to a figure of $2.1 trillion for 2007. Even if the annual increment could be held to only 6%, the total medical bill will rise from today's frightening $1+ trillion to a nightmare $16 trillion by 2050. Worse, nobody seems really happy with the system this amazing price will produce. The building is decaying rapidly and repair efforts are failing.

HOW IT ALL HAPPENED

The point: Medicine is now in an unacceptable state because of efforts to control cost. The cause of cost was free spending. The cause of free spending was mistaken thinking by our leadership, in which the principles of ordinary human behavior were ignored. To shift metaphors, the lid was left off the cookie jar at the Cub Scout meeting, the jar is almost empty, and the alarmed parents have now called 911.

THE STARTER (THE TRAGIC FLAW)

How did it happen? The process is not mysterious. And we should have known.

It is the early 1940's. Defense contractors are desperate for more employees. Most of the young men have gone to war. Wages are frozen. Women (like "Rosie the Riveter") are just now coming into the manual labor workforce. Industry appeals to Congress to allow employers — but not employees — to deduct from taxable income any funds paid for workers' health benefits. Suddenly health insurance is "free" to the man or woman on the assembly line. Congress seems to think that the patient, the doctor, and the hospital will not vary their behavior based on funding. They think the patient will go to the doctor just as often whether she is paying for it or not. The doctor will order the same tests and procedures and hospitalization, never mind who's paying. The hospital will set its room rates and its payrolls each year without checking what the market will bear. Medicine, alone of all commodities, is somehow immune to economic principles; Congressional edict has suspended the laws of human nature. Thus: the Tragic Flaw — the error in reasoning which has brought us to this unfortunate place. To compound this conceptual flight of fancy, the average insurance company now agrees to pay 80% of going charges ("usual and customary fees"), whatever they are. Is it a surprise that going charges shot up every year?

THE ENABLER (THE GRAND DISGUISE)

When Congress passes — and President Roosevelt signs — this bill in 1943, they don't, of course, provide employees with free health benefits; they only disguise them. The average American's yearly salary in 1945 is now around $2000 (!).*The new federal bill permits employers to add a typical $150 for health insurance — a sum which is not, in general, even revealed to the worker. Rosie the Riveter and her peers get a 7.5% raise and don't know it. More importantly, they are not allowed to control it — are not allowed to save it, spend it, pay off their mortgage. It is already spent, so make the best of it.

THE ACCELERATOR (THE BIG BANG)

It is now 1965: the Congress and the executive branch become remorseful — not over what they have done but over what they have left out. They have not taken care of the retired folks. Here are the over-65 group — with no job, rapidly climbing health needs, and no health insurance. So a new concept emerges

---

*Compare with $34,000 salary and $5000 health benefits in 1994 . In 1945, 5%; in 1994, 13%. This reflects only the worker's contribution — the true per-capita cost: in 1994 this was about $4220; in 1960, it was close to $141.

with the Social Security Bill of 1965: Medicare. The federal government will now "award" the same benefits to the elderly that the younger set were "given." Here again, it prints up no fixed schedule of payments — it will pay 80% of whatever charges happen to be incurred in the doctor's office or hospital. Will there be a tendency for charges to go up in this open-ended system? Will there be a trend toward more procedures? more visits? History provides the answer.

Interestingly, if one looks at a chart spanning this century, health costs closely paralleled inflation from 1900 until 1970, at which point medical expenditures took off almost exponentially, rising not 3-10% per year like the Consumer Price Index but 14-22% per year. The health bill in 1960 was $27 billion; in 1997 a little over $1 trillion — CPI up about 6 times, medicine up 40 times. The "Big Bang" had now occurred, and Medicare had ignited it. Government and industry together had unintentionally begun to issue unlimited blank checks to provider and consumer and then provide no supervision for the check-writing. The sky literally was the limit, and no one knew where the universe ended. The only other precedent in American history for such an extravagant act was perhaps the status of the defense contractors in World War II. Nothing was too good. And nothing ever got so expensive. Medical people profited significantly from

Medicare — for now they were paid for services they had previously performed *pro bono* or at a discount. Nonetheless organized medicine, typified by the American Medical Association (AMA), can claim credit for at least initially opposing the legislation, saying that "It would put the government into the practice of medicine."

THE PERPETUATOR (THE ZOOM FACTOR)

Provided with the blank checks of "free" (disguised) insurance and Medicare (costs still hidden), the spending spree started. But not without help. The honey pot was attractive, and bureaucrats, entrepreneurs, and consultants have swarmed.

Creative accounting by some hospitals, some doctors, some drug houses, and some equipment manufacturers became routine.

Unbundling — in which the hospital business office no longer charged for "daily care" but listed each bar of soap and disposable bedpan — swelled the "Total" line of every hospital bill.

Biomedical *research* and the technological advances it spawned, desirable though they certainly were, made everything cost more. Once you can image every nook and cranny of the brain painlessly with a CT scan or MRI ($700-1200 a shot), can you go back to crude skull films, inconvenient arteriograms, or medieval-seeming brain air studies? If aminoglycosides ($80-100 a day) are marvelous solutions to certain ("gram-negative") infections, will the doctor or patient be content with the plodding but cheap sulfa drugs ($3/day)?

Federal money poured into medical development: the '60's was widely known among researchists as the honeymoon decade. With "wonder drugs" and amazing surgery came *unrealistic promises* — everything can be cured and everybody should have access to the best. Public expectations surpassed reality; the demand spiraled upwards and, according to the economics equation, so did cost.

Meanwhile, to further swell this demand, the *population base* expanded massively with that demographic explosion called the "baby boom." Number of people in the U. S. in 1950: 130 million; number in 1996: 260 million.

The *supply of physicians* climbed even faster, from about 220,000 in 1950 to 800,000 in 1996; economist Eli Ginsberg* suggested that each new doctor causes a $1,000,000 yearly expenditure.

A large and overlooked, if incalculable, part of

---

*He even made the tongue-in-cheek proposal in 1984 that the government offer every medical student $250,000 to terminate his enrollment and drop out of medical school.

the cost zoom factor is what may be termed *medical shoplifting*. Anyone who appears at the emergency room with anything from a cold to a major surgical crisis must, by federal law, be treated — and treated on site. A person who is not financially able to buy coverage and is not on Medicaid or Medicare — or even someone who chooses not to buy health insurance, preferring, let's say, a new bass boat — can stroll into any private ER and receive standard care, including hospitalization if needed. He or she cannot be ferried to a nearby public facility — on pain of punishment of the institution and doctors under COBRA provisions.* The patient, meanwhile, may have no plan to pay the bill if it comes. He/she has shoplifted and, as with the department store, other customers pay the freight (estimated to be 10% in the retail world; no good figures are available in the medical field but must be significant).

Inflation — at times excessive — did its part: the salaries of office personnel went up; hospital workers became more precious as minimum wage figures

---

*A genuine irony in this area was the passage of a proposition in California two years ago which provided for illegal aliens (almost all of whom have no insurance and no money) not to receive state health benefits whenever they presented to hospitals. That's only fair, right? These people are stealing from citizens, right? The problem: federal law requires the hospital to treat them, so the new state law now punishes the hospital, not the illicit alien.

climbed; a piece of equipment — say, a table — was priced four times as high if it could be labeled a "medical" item.

Medical *malpractice* costs skyrocketed. Since everybody should now be cured, and since every doctor and hospital had deep-pocket insurance (grandly disguised!), maybe you should sue for every bad result. Is death only natural, or is it a medical mistake? The average internist's liability premium in 1950 was $50, and many didn't even bother to have insurance; in 1998, it is in the $5200 range, and he can't even get on a hospital staff without it. The neurosurgeon's tab rose over the same period from a negligible level in 1950 to about $15,600 in 1982 and to an average $34,000 in 1998. Some are much higher. The malpractice industry is thought to cost $100 billion per year, but this number doesn't include the incalculable expenditure generated by the physician's fear of being sued. How many defensive tests does he order? How many consultations? How much extra time does he spend documenting every encounter? This figure has been variously estimated, but some would place it at 35% of the total $1+ trillion.

The role of *entrepreneurism* probably should not be minimized, either: consultants, seminars, advertising abound. Contracting organizations for every discipline — urology, neurosurgery, cardiology — have sprouted everywhere. The typical physician's office mail contains six-inch stacks of expensive four-color brochures, destined only to enrich the "circular file."

Another inestimable cost is that of conforming to *bureaucratization*. Meeting OSHA guidelines has been thought to run $15,000 per office. Documenting and billing and explaining for Medicare probably adds a new employee ($40,000) and perhaps a new computer system ($50-100,000) for each three doctors. Dealing with 30-50 separate insurance and HMO programs generates unknown but significant, perhaps massive, cost.

But, you say, think of all the progress in medicine: coronary bypass, joint replacement, drug therapy for every condition. And, furthermore, no other rapidly-advancing industry has been immune to these forces, has it? Well, the technologic explosion in the electronic business is interesting. It too has zoomed, but the word processor on which this paper is being composed, though greatly improved over the last 15 years, now costs less, not more.

You see, the money is mine. And the price I pay for my computer is not disguised.

THE GOLDEN LOAF

In what already appears to be a surreal situation, a fairy tale may be useful. Once upon a time, the Kingdom of Christopher got into a terrible war. To attract workers, industry decided to provide bread, that essential item, to employees, "as needed." The companies — but not the employees — got permission from the King and Parliament to deduct the cost from taxable income. No rate sheet was printed up. The company bought bread "insurance" to provide 80% of the going rate. Many times, the grocery store would "accept" the insurance rate and not insist on collecting the remaining 20%.

Meantime, the King and the Parliament were watching. Soon, instead of becoming alarmed that an uncontrolled market situation was developing, they decided to give the over-65 population the same break the working people had. After all, bread was the staff of life, wasn't it? Anybody over 65 could have all the bread they "needed" — they paid only 20%, the "government" (taxpayer) supplied the other 80%. Bread became the staple of the elderly. Consumer and provider found no limits on the consumption, production, cost, or volume of bread. So as growers, brokers, manufacturers, and retail outlets understood the opportunity, the price of bread kept climbing. Soon

80% of the new price was many times the total old price. Bakers made fancier bread. They enriched it with all kinds of vitamins and minerals. Families stormed the supermarkets for bread and the lines kept getting longer — after all, it was "free," right?

What happened to the price of bread in the Land of Christopher? It zoomed. Now, after half a century, no one in the Land can possibly afford bread unless he or she is "covered" by an employer plan or "Medibread." Economists and candidates for office and journalists throughout the Land loudly complain that 17% of the population has no bread insurance and can't afford bread out of pocket. Loaves of enriched sourdough are displayed in bakers' windows — glistening with a golden patina, bearing a price tag no one is willing, or able, to pay. Industry is cutting deals with food brokers, insisting on simpler fare and lower prices, capitating their bread budgets. The King's government, fearful that Medibread will be bankrupt by 2005, schedules cuts in bread deliveries and steps up payments by individual citizens. The public and press complain loudly about the quality of bread, worry about having to pay more out of pocket, insist that having free bread is their right. Some members of the RightWing party say drastic cuts will be necessary to save the system, while LeftWingers criticize them for being mean-spirited and "taking your Medibread benefits away." Polls indicate the people want to hear any story which is reassuring.

Told that access to bread is worse and the quality of bread is going down, the government adopts elaborate rules to "control" bread-making practices. Fines and other penalties are imposed by Parliament on bakers if clerks think the manufacturing process isn't as outlined in a 400-page coding manual put together jointly by the Christopher Bakers' Association and the Bread Financing Council. The King appoints a blue-ribbon panel to study and create a document on people's bread rights. By now, because of the way the government financed food, the citizens of the Land of Christopher are learning to make stone soup.

And the citizens of America are feeling the drafts coming through the crevices in the walls of their defective building.

HOW OTHERS DO IT

We must, then, contract for another building venture. But surely we should be able to learn from others. Surely some other nation, struggling with this problem, has succeeded.

Actually, as the teenagers say, *not.* There is an extensive literature on healthcare systems across the globe, but a brief current update goes something like this. The *British system,* with its national health service, permits access (if you have all day) to a physician encounter which most Americans would consider a five- and dimestore event. Serious problems are referred, but important therapies like hip reconstruction and surgery for prostate cancer may be delayed for a year or more. Costs and dissatisfaction are mounting and one of the fast growing industries in England is now private health insurance.

The *German sickness fund* concept, with primary care physicians seeing 70 or more patients a day from 8 a.m. to 10 p.m., is getting costly too, and doctors have been disaffecting for years.

The much-touted (not lately!) Canadian system, with set payments but uncontrolled volume, is threatening to bankrupt some provinces, and managed care is moving in. Meanwhile, of course, the delays for critical procedures like cardiac revascularization have resulted in 25% mortality from time of diagnosis in some places (compare 1.5% in the U. S.) and have also provoked migration across the border at an alarming pace (by the way, these major costs are not usually figured in the estimates of Canadian health expenditures).

There are, of course, plenty of advocates in the U. S. for a "single-payer system" (*read:* the government pays; *translate:* the citizen still pays), and there are those who confidently predict that such a federal program will be next. Even the American College of Surgeons, faced with the risks of capitation, tentatively offered a proposal which favored such a plan. The majority of the mainstream press seems quietly confident the government will take over. Even The Defend Health Care movement, mainly doctors, in Massachusetts seems to applaud the concept. The editor of a major professional journal in a speech before a medical school group thought the Clinton plan was "not bad." The other nations, clearly, have experienced their own versions of the classic mistakes: the Tragic Flaw in reasoning which presumes an unvarying level of medical care and the Grand Disguise of removing personal responsibility for cost. Santayana warned that he who forgets the mistakes of history is destined to repeat them. The mistakes in healthcare are on display — is it really necessary for us to do these experiments over?

BACK UP THE YELLOW BRICK ROAD

About the time this process started in the 40's, the motion picture Wizard of Oz was very popular. When Dorothy, her puppy Toto, and her bizarre friends discovered that Oz was a fake fantasy land and the Wizard was a confidence man (the same old snake-oil salesman from back home), they made a rational decision: Go back up the yellow brick road to Kansas and learn to deal once again with reality.

What about us: Is there hope? Can we go back up the road? Is there a way to correct these errors of process which were created by ignoring the rules of human motivation? Logic would say yes: The system is the problem; so change the system. . . gradually.

All goods, services, and commodities are, of course, rationed — by availability and cost. You and I do not eat caviar and lobster every day — they're too expensive. We don't live in Bill Gates' house — it's horrendously extravagant. We don't wear Ralph Lauren garments to dig in the garden — too pricy. And we don't sit around and complain that these basics — food, shelter, clothing — are thereby unfairly rationed.

Further, we all know, of course, that medical care, necessary as it is, is not as critical as other commodities, like food or shelter. Everyone knows people who have survived well without medical attention for half a century; no one survives without food for half a month. One wonders why, then, medical care has been moved up the ladder of the public agenda, leapfrogging more basic concerns. It's time to remove the mask: everything is rationed. Rationing is essential. Rationing is rational. The question is: Who does it?

In the 1930's, every family paid its own health bill. The doctor and the patient, facing a decision, both motivated to be prudent, sat down and decided what was needed, what was reasonable, and what was afford-able. My father, practicing 1926-1966 (he missed Medicare!), was limited in what was available, but was dedicated to quality and had every incentive to be care-ful of his patient's pocketbook. So did the hospital administrator. So did the drug maker.

In the last 30 years, things have been different. The doctor has been rewarded for over-utilization — for hospitalizing patients, for scheduling surgery, bring-ing the patient back more often, ordering more tests in his office. The patient didn't mind — as a matter of fact, was anxious to get the most out of available bene-fits, paid (it seemed) by another. The more a hospital or drug manufacturer charged, the more they got — from the insurance company or the government. Before the payers caught on, patients requested hospi-talization "so the insurance will pay." During my prac-tice years, 1962 through the present, I have been encouraged by the system not to worry, or even think about, cost. Had I been an efficient entrepreneur, I suppose I would have wanted to pump up expendi-tures.

My son, who started practice in 1989, faces a still different prospect. Now the rationing will be done by the wrong people — not by him and not by his patients but by personnel with clerical or administrative assignments and a nearly complete ignorance of the discipline they are regulating.

My father and his patient were prudent; my patient and I were spendthrift; my son and his patient will be told what to do by people without training and without any acquaintance with the individual "consumer's" situation.

NOW WHAT? — A GRADUAL 50-YEAR PLAN

We have, of course, two problems: first, our people have become convinced that the health care dollar materializes out of nowhere and they should never have to pay — they are now addicts to medical paternalism. This first problem, of course, is the Grand Disguise incarnate. I spoke to a Medicare-age audience recently and pointed out that, "All of you in this room want all the people in the next room to pay your health bill. But — all the people in the next room want you to pay theirs." The real fact is: If your employer "provides" health insurance, you are still paying for your own coverage and also for the health bills of the uninsured, like it or not. The same is true of Medicare: you're paying for it (and, ironically, if you're too young to use it, you will pay more). Shouldn't you have some say on how it is spent?

Second, our political representatives have an operative horizon which extends a year or two; asked to initiate a 50-year process, they turn their thoughts to the election coming up in 18 months. But our elected lawmakers will eventually do what they think you insist on. If you decide the light has been turned on, and the only way for your grandchildren to get reasonable healthcare is to start a long-term reality process, they will respond. But can we change our thinking? Can our addiction be cured? History answers. Remember when women couldn't vote? Remember slavery? Horrific predictions of what would happen with correction of these injustices did not materialize. The "third rail" that is supposed to be healthcare we can similarly de-electrify.

Stripping the mask of the Grand Disguise and correcting the Tragic Flaw will involve gradually returning the husbandry of the healthcare dollar to the citizen. Getting where we are now has required a half-century; the road back must be as long. We cannot, in other words, tear the house down as a first step. Like Descartes, as he erected a new system on his single precept — *"Cogito, ergo sum"* ("I think, therefore I am") — we will need a nice, conventional residence, someplace to live while the new structure is being built.

A number of measures, some already proposed, should work, and it would be refreshing to witness a debate in Congress dealing with the following reality-oriented considerations rather than the tentative public-opinion-water-testing process which has been going on so far.

I. THE WORKING POPULATION

These options, primarily applicable to commercial health coverage, are here designated modules because they are not mutually exclusive but can be combined to form a coherent plan. Medicare is discussed separately (II).

Module A - Level the playing field. Provide a stepwise method, over years, to allow employees like employers a tax credit on their health insurance premiums. Then they become decision-makers instead of passive recipients.

For example, a typical head of household with a wife and one child is presently earning $36,000, but really earns $39,600 — the $3600 is sequestered away (grandly disguised) to pay for his medical plan. If he received the money to purchase his own health insurance under current laws he would pay full income taxes on the $3600. If on the other hand he were granted the same "break" as his employer — and allowed to deduct up to $3600 from taxable income — he could control his own medical life. First, he would purchase obligatory major medical benefits (see below) with, say, a $2000-$3000 deductible for about $800-1200 per year. He would then have the choice of buying other health coverage through a group arrangement with the remaining $2600, or pay medical expenses as they appear. All monies spent on health care including documented incidental expenses up to the $3600 ceiling would be deductible. It is not difficult to imagine the prudence he — and especially his wife — would show in doling out dollars for medical care: they would carefully consider the need for an MRI now that the costs are real.

The medical savings account, or medical IRA, is closely related (see below). A proposal to allow 100% deductibility for the "self-employed" proprietor had passed as part of a bill in the House of Representatives at publication time but faced an uncertain future in the Senate and a likely presidential veto.

Module B - Gradually raise co-pay. Some companies have progressively increased employee participation so that now the individual pays as much as 50% of his own health premiums. The managers say that not only have company expenses gone down from the shifting of costs, the employees are more prudent with their utilization of the system. A variation of this plan would be to continue the shift over a couple of decades — gradually pass all costs to the employee but make the second 50% — or even the entire amount — tax-deductible (see Module A).

Module C- Reward frugality. A few firms have instituted a plan of bonuses to employees who control their health costs, with the parent company remaining "self-insured." Expenditures have dropped steadily. One might postulate there might be a risk of minimizing care, but those using this system say only trivial expenses disappear — important care is delivered anyway.

Module D - Establish fixed rate schedules and allow balance billing. That is, let the payer — commercial or public, HMO or insurance company, self-insured employer or employer-cooperative — state what it will pay and the patient, doctor, hospital will make their own arrangements for any balance. Then the patient exercises her shopping skills, can look around and take the best deal. The old costly system of providing 80% of "whatever" will have evaporated, and the stepwise inflationary effect of the "usual and customary rate" will disappear.

Module E - Permit discounts. At the moment it is against the law for a doctor to discount the Medicare patient's 20% payment for any reason (or, for that matter, to give other doctors professional discounts which eliminate co-pay or the extra 20%) without pursuing the balance rigorously. The Inspector General has even set up a hot line to detect such infractions. If balance billing is allowed, then reducing or wiping clean the balance will also be permitted: a salutary effect on prices should ensue.

Module F - Promote Medical Savings Accounts. These funds, consisting of tax-deferred savings, will provide for major medical policies (see below), and the remainder can either be used for lesser medical expenses or for health insurance, or, if not spent, will accumulate, along with tax-deferred compound interest, toward a retirement fund. The present "experiment" allowing recipients to use these tax-deferred "IRAs" to pay their medical bills has not blossomed as hoped by some but has not yet been tested in the real market. For one thing, the tentativeness with which the government permitted this limited test model (about three-quarters of a million instances) is discouraging to insurance companies; entrepreneurism, with its inherent capital risks, does not flourish in an "iffy" environment. Furthermore, the persistence of the seemingly "magic" Big-Brother alternative, still offered, is hard to abandon (even though our Big Brother is, of all people, *us*).

Radical changes in our concepts are long overdue, anyway. It is most reasonable to view ordinary health coverage as not being insurance at all. The usual "bets" we make with insurance companies about whether we will die, or whether our house will burn down, are rational because neither the insured nor the insurer want the event to happen. The same is true with major medical coverage: no one would want to cash in on a policy which applies only to prolonged hospitalization or incarceration in an intensive care unit. But everyone wants to "use" her day-to-day coverage for office visits. So anything below, say, $2000 a year is pre-paid care, not insurance at all. No wonder it's so dear. Think of the people owning the "bread insurance" previously referred to in the fairy tale: how often would the benefits be used up?

Module G - Provide Vouchers for Indigents. Patients with incomes below certain pre-determined levels currently either access public medical/hospital facilities according to local city, county, or authority provisions; go to public or private facilities where their (state) Medicaid plan is accepted; or, if not covered by Medicaid or Medicare, use facilities where they receive charity care. Because they may have no regular physician, ordinary ailments trigger much more expensive visits to emergency rooms. If they were given vouchers, specifically redeemable by certified insurance companies, HMOs, or medical provider groups — but not cashable otherwise — economically feasible coverage could be provided. "Risk" plans would undoubtedly result: community hospitals, now struggling for survival in many areas, could offer global plans based on acceptance of annual vouchers, rather than the present situation of providing care which is posted in the books but never compensated. The vouchers could be funded by federal and state monies currently routed to Medicaid; unlike the latter, a definite cap would automatically be placed on expenditures and realistic budgets could be put together.

Module H - Require Major-Medical Policies. All citizens would be obligated to own an approved high-deductible (perhaps $2000) policy with a certified insurance company, institution, consortium, or HMO, if only to protect the rest of the public from medical shoplifting and from the indirect cost flow from prolonged hospitalization of individuals with no coverage. This rule would be analogous, then, to the seat-belt law: at least shield others from the huge costs of a severe accident or catastrophic illness, just as obligatory seat restraints protect the uninvolved population from the costs of trauma management.

II. THE ELDERLY POPULATION

The Problem

Medicare, on its 33rd anniversary, is a promissory note dangled tentatively before the eyes of the American people. By 2001, there will be no "Medicare Fund," secured from harm, prudently invested, earning useful amounts of interest. There will be only a con-

71

duit: Medicare benefits are already paid mainly from the current flux of general taxes, and the enormous annual invoice of $300 billion is being met, fortuitously, by the high productivity of the big under-65 population. This huge sum is in turn being spent by the smaller over-65 group without serious regard for, or clear knowledge of, its source.

This lucky circumstance which currently sustains Medicare will soon reverse itself. Congressional leaders and the Office of the Budget variously estimate that the program will "go bankrupt" by 2005, or 2010. This statement is itself an irony: it implies that the program is now secure when, in fact, Medicare is only tenuously balanced on the fence of demographic circumstance. The population surge called the Baby Boom is responsible. There are more people aged 38 than any other single age with the spread of the bulge ranging from 30 to 52, and this statistical reality will soon move like a standing wave through age 65, producing a simultaneous triple economic upheaval:

Upheaval #1: The Boom people will leave their productive period and stop or reduce tax payments to the Medicare conduit.

Upheaval #2: They — more of them than ever in history — will suddenly qualify for and start receiving Medicare benefits.

Upheaval #3: They will pass through the looking-glass into an age group in which medical costs are easily five times what they were previously.

The vigorous producer suddenly becomes an avid consumer; a barely self-supporting operation becomes a big cost center.

Looking for answers

Above age 65, today's American who is not employed full time cannot get primary health insurance outside of Medicare. This amazing fact is not known to most; a working person suddenly discovers that his non-working spouse, newly 65, has been unceremoniously dropped from the company medical benefits program, usually without notification. She's uninsured and has been for six months! She hasn't applied for Medicare, thinking she was still covered by "the company store." And depending on her birthday and the time of year, she may be unable to secure Medicare Part B (Part A is usually quicker) for months or even a year.

Even if health insurance were available, it would likely be unaffordable, since vigilant insurance actuaries are fully aware of the risks of becoming "elderly." The older population quintuples the expenses of the younger generations — insurance rates if calculated would be immense. This huge disproportion is in large part attributable to the end-of-life phenomenon: the dying patient is sustained in the hospital, the intensive care unit, and/or the skilled nursing facility for weeks or months. The cost datum here is incredible: 80% of expenses are consumed in the last few months of life. This is the age group of course in which death is most likely to occur and, it turns out, death in America is terribly expensive.

Recognizing as they must these hard facts, our elected representatives only gingerly dare to touch the "electrified third rail" of Medicare (or, for that matter, Social Security) because the public signals through polls and on election day their horror at reduced benefits, increased deductibles, introduction of a co-pay, or increased taxes, when common sense would seem to beg for enactment of all four. Our congressional representatives on the conservative side view the situation with alarm, announce a crisis, and maintain that the other party is at fault. Meantime the liberal contingent suggest that even a mention of these realities is cruel and unfriendly.

The vehicle bids fair to stall on its tracks because neither party is courageous enough to touch the dangerous third rail and deal with reality. Perhaps, before the electricity stops for good, we should consider reengineering the power plant.

A Workable Solution

In creating a new algorithm for eldercare, in which the principle of economic self-management is re-introduced, it seems prudent to bear in mind four elements:

(1) Eighty per cent of taxes — including those used to sustain the Medicare program — are paid by 20% of the population;

(2) The costs — as well as insurance coverage — of eldercare have skyrocketed beyond the means of many as a result of the Grand Disguise and its equally illogical sister-concepts (including the Tragic Flaw and the Zoom Factor);

(3) Several administrative strata must be accepted (there are already many). The two mechanisms called into play would logically be a tax credit and a voucher.

(4) Major-medical, or catastrophic, coverage must be mandatory (see above) in order to protect the healthcare system as well as taxpayers from the impact of huge, unpredictable, and otherwise uncompensated bills.

Also, as one starts the building process, it may be informative to look at the Medicare capitation system already in place (Medicare HMOs). Here the government awards to some provider system the total responsibility for medical care of an over-65 person in return for a standard premium which has been calculated on the basis of average expenditures in the area. These vary from as low as $385 to as high as $600 per member per month in different sections of the country. Only some 6-7% of Medicare beneficiaries are currently enrolled in these programs (and the votes are not yet in on quality or viability — insurance companies are dropping the contracts more rapidly than others are taking them up), but if all Medicare patients were handled this way, one could calculate the annual bill easily: $500 per month x 12 = $6000 per year x 40 million = $240 billion — quite a bit less than the present cost, making the concept appealing to HCFA economists.

If then a means test is applied, based on data already available through the internal revenue system, beneficiaries can be awarded a tax credit if they pay enough taxes or a health voucher if they do not. Here, as before, a several-decade phase-in program would be practical and palatable.

Module A - The Tax Credit Stratum. Individuals who pay, say, $12,000 or more in annual federal income taxes (annual income $50,000 or more) would be granted a $6000 break. They would then be required to purchase an approved major-medical health policy (cost $1500-2500 per year, with about $2000-5000 of benefits deductible). The rest they could use to obtain a standard preventive policy to cover part of the deductible and other costs through their associa-

76

tion pool or other purchasing consortium. Or, alternatively, they could put aside these funds, invested tax-free, and use them as needed for month-to-month health expenses. Or they can save or use them for other discretionary purposes. It is easy to see that the incentive to become a serious healthcare shopper and to not spend these funds casually would be substantial. It is also easy to see that providers would arrange to offer attractive packages of good services at good prices.

Module B - The Health Voucher Stratum. People whose household income is insufficient to allow them the "privilege" of paying income taxes to the federal government — those with incomes below about $18,000 per year — would be granted a federal voucher for health services, approximately equivalent to $6000 in purchasing power. This certificate would be redeemable only by presenting it to a private or public, but federally approved, health provider system — "charity" hospital, insurance company, HMO, provider group, vertically integrated system — who would in turn be responsible for global provision of services: major medical, drugs, surgery, preventive care, etc. The beneficiary of the voucher would thus have the opportunity to shop the mall and pick the booth which appears to provide the most, and the best, services. Competition would mount, but not competition for price — competition for quality of program within predetermined fiscal limits.

Module C - The Intermediate Stratum. These citizens pay taxes, but only in the $5,000-11,000 per year range. They would be granted an intermediate voucher, worth about $3000, which would be used for the mandatory major medical policy plus a basic supplementary program. They would also be granted an additional $3000 tax credit which, like Module A people, they can use as they choose — purchase more insurance, pay health expenses as they go, or put the money aside as savings or even discretionary income. A sliding scale could obviously be substituted for this category, but might be too cumbersome.

Among the advantages of such a proposal would be the fact that it would not discourage continued productive wage earning after age 65 as Social Security does. As things now stand, the qualified SS beneficiary cannot receive payments from age 65 through 69 if earned income exceeds a small maximum — encouraging him or her to stop work, stop paying taxes, and receive a check from the government. Here the citizen could continue productive endeavors, make a good income, and get the same break that everyone else does.

In the new system doctors and hospitals can charge whatever they wish and discount whatever they wish — *if the customer agrees to the price.* Competition

— and the doctor-patient negotiation — will suddenly control the day. Thus, with patients in Module B, providers will likely "accept" the standard payment schedule of the insurance company or health system; some will have signed up as part of a vertical system, as they do now. If not, the customer can shop for a provider who will. Customers in Modules A or B will shop as well, but they have the choice of negotiating or paying the going rate of a doctor or hospital they choose.

In the case of the voucher patient, the government continues to serve as a conduit, but with the element of predictability and control introduced. In the case of the tax-credit patient, the government serves as an enabler, allowing people to pay their own bills from monies already collected by the government but strategically veiled.

An additional benefit will surface: it will now be unnecessary to employ so many agents of the Office of Inspector General, the Federal Bureau of Investigation, and the Health Care Financing Administration — there will now be 40 million unpaid individual patrolmen of the process, husbanding their own funds, making their own decisions, controlling costs. Various claims made regarding "Medicare fraud" — $10 billion? $23 billion? — will become moot. The vast expensive bureaucratic process deployed to rout it out will no longer be a burden on the public — or even needed.

And the Grand Disguise will have vanished.

THE VIEW FROM 2050

What, then, will be the fate of medicine over the next half-century? Will a government-sponsored, fatally extravagant program emerge? Will rationing of expensive procedures by committee-consensus appear state by state? Knowledgeable and intellectual visionaries like William B. Schwartz, MD, hope for virtual elimination, at mid-century, of major disease processes by means of human genomic adjustment and other molecular biologic manipulation. Such a consummation — devoutly wished for though it may be — would doubtless require huge economic commitments for research and massive appropriations for application of the techniques discovered at a time when the mere delivery of routine services has brought healthcare to its fiscal knees. Meanwhile, what of the new diseases which emerge as others are subdued? Will unrecognized defective genes, previously made moot by the lethal expressions of those known, then show their heads? Each quantum advance in medicine has, alas, generated a new series of unpredicted problems — like the weird infections in people on chemotherapy, like the whole new range of diagnoses in patients receiving organ transplants. Will gene transformation be any different?

If nothing substantive is done, we shall continue repairing and patching. We shall encourage managed care, then make laws which prevent it from working. We shall foster, then decry, the HMOs and wish for the old days. We shall move toward single-payer programs and watch the Grand Disguise expand. We shall magnify government surveillance (by non-medical people) at great cost and great distress to the healthcare profession and the people it serves. We shall extend the curve of medical inflation, so that, at present rates, it will have grown over the next half-century from an already insupportable to a then inconceivable level. Access to care will get worse, not better. We shall be unable to eat the golden loaf. We will go from trouble to disaster.

The healthcare situation in America brings to mind Poe's *Masque of the Red Death:* The disguises fell away only as the plague descended. We need the dance director to call now for removal of the masks before we are consumed. We need for him to announce, "Ladies and gentlemen, the costume ball is over."

If indeed we can proceed with a plan for returning the management of the healthcare dollar to the individual, reason will have been introduced; personal cost will help govern decisions; providers will compete to reduce, not pad, prices. Medicine perhaps will not be as remunerative to the "providers" as it has been over the last half-century but it will have regained a semblance of reality.

If we sit down once again to the drawing board of our new house; if this time we use common sense; and if we do not pretend that the laws of human nature have been repealed, the new structure will be sound. The health bill will have increased only slowly, slower than general inflation, and, though still large, will have shrunk relative to the GDP — down from 14%, down perhaps to four or five percent. Down where we can live with it. Down where the powerful housewife knows the tab, spends her own money, and controls the cost. Where our grandchildren can get good care for a decent price.

And where they, and their doctors, can make the health decisions.

Sources

IN THIS PAPER, THE AUTHOR HAS LIBERALLY
DRAWN FROM MANY PEOPLE AND PLACES, SUCH AS:

The Advisory Board; Kaufmann Consultants; Hamilton-KSA;
The Sharp System of Health Care; a Georgia Power executive;
PROMINA Board Members, executives and staff; Piedmont
Medical Center Board; ACP Colleagues; HCFA Bulletins; Pub-
lications of Office of Budget and Management; Georgia State
Business School; Malcolm Forbes; George Gilder; Rep. Newt
Gingrich; Sen. Daniel Patrick Moynihan; T. S. Eliot; Santayana;
Descartes; Schopenhauer; Goethe; Henry Ford; The Holy
Bible; Lincoln; Emerson; Karl Marx; Yogi Berra; William B.
Schwartz, MD; Wall Street Journal and Wall Street Journal
Almanac; New York Times; American Medical News; Medical
Economics; The Federal Register: Tax Bill of 1943, Soc Securi-
ty Act of 1965,The Kassebaum-Kennedy Bill; Edgar Allan Poe;
Colleagues; Employees; Patients; Medical School Faculties;
Alexis de Toqueville; Saint Paul Insurance Company; MAG
Mutual Insurance Co.; Law firm of Long, Weinberg; Aetna;
Blue Choice; Cigna; US HealthCare; United HealthCare; Pru-
dential; Kaiser-Permanente System; and many others .